C0-BIJ-649

Contents

Boldface words appear in the glossary.

Elephant Estimation

Estimating means using facts to make a guess about something. You can estimate about elephants in this book! Check your answers on page 22.

Look at the elephants on the next page. Without counting each one, are there more or fewer than 10 elephants?

ANIMAL MATH

ESTIMATING WITH ELEPHANTS

By Rory McDonnell

Gareth Stevens
PUBLISHING

Leveled Reader math

Please visit our website, www.garethstevens.com. For a free color catalog of all our high-quality books, call toll free 1-800-542-2595 or fax 1-877-542-2596.

Cataloging-in-Publication Data

Names: McDonnell, Rory.
Title: Estimating with elephants / Rory McDonnell.
Description: New York : Gareth Stevens Publishing, 2018. | Series: Animal math | Includes index.
Identifiers: ISBN 9781538208489 (pbk.) | ISBN 9781538208496 (library bound) | ISBN 9781538208519 (6 pack)
Subjects: LCSH: Estimation theory–Juvenile literature. | Elephants–Juvenile literature.
Classification: LCC QA276.8 M35545 2018 | DDC 519.5'44–dc23

Published in 2018 by
Gareth Stevens Publishing
111 East 14th Street, Suite 349
New York, NY 10003

Copyright © 2018 Gareth Stevens Publishing

Designer: Sarah Liddell
Editor: Therese Shea

Photo credits: Cover, p. 1 Nuamfolio/Shutterstock.com; background used throughout T. Sumaetho/Shutterstock.com; p. 5 David Steele/Shutterstock.com; p. 7 venusvi/Shutterstock.com; p. 9 Michael Potter11/Shutterstock.com; p. 11 GUDKOV ANDREY/Shutterstock.com; p. 13 Luca Nichetti/Shutterstock.com; p. 15 Emma Geary/Shutterstock.com; p. 17 Eakachai Leesin/Shutterstock.com; p. 19 Hajakely/Shutterstock.com; p. 21 JOHNATHAN PLEDGER/Shutterstock.com.

Printed in China

CPSIA compliance information: Batch #CW18GS: For further information contact Gareth Stevens, New York, New York at 1-800-542-2595.

Living Large

There are three **species** of elephants. An Asian elephant can be as tall as 10 feet (3 m) from the ground to its shoulder.

Look at the next page. Which is the best estimate for how tall the elephant is in real life, 9 feet or 9 inches?

The African savanna elephant is the largest elephant! It can be as tall as 13 feet (4 m) from the ground to its shoulder.

Look at the next page. Which is the best estimate for how tall the elephant is in real life, 4 centimeters or 4 meters?

The African forest elephant is another species. All African elephants have larger ears than Asian elephants. Their ears keep them cool in the hot sun.

Look at the ruler and the elephant on the next page. Which is the best estimate for how tall the elephant is, 8 feet or 16 feet?

4 feet

Baby Elephants!

Even baby elephants, or calves, are large. They suck their trunk just like human babies suck their thumb!

Look at the ruler and the elephant calf on the next page. Which is the best estimate for how tall the calf is, 3 feet or 6 feet?

1 foot

Terrific Tusks and Trunks

Male African and Asian elephants often have two **tusks**. Female African elephants have tusks, too. Most female Asian elephants don't.

Look at the ruler and the elephant calf's tusk on the next page. Estimate how many inches long the calf's tusk is.

I 1 inch

15

An elephant's trunk is like a long nose and lip together! Trunks are for smelling, picking up and holding things, and drinking water.

Look at the ruler and the elephant's trunk on the next page. Estimate how many meters long the elephant's trunk is.

1 meter

Huge Herds

Elephants live in groups. Groups can form a herd of up to 40 elephants.

There were 8 elephants. Then, 9 elephants joined them. Estimate the total number of elephants. Round each number below to the nearest ten. Add the rounded numbers.

$$8 + 9$$

Elephant herds walk a lot looking for plants to eat. Herds **protect** weaker elephants from lions. Elephants are amazing animals!

There were 11 elephants. Then, 18 elephants joined them. Estimate the total number of elephants. Round each number below to the nearest ten. Add the rounded numbers.

$$11 + 18$$

Glossary

protect: to keep something from being harmed

species: a group of animals that are alike and can produce young animals

tusk: a very long, large tooth that sticks out of the mouth of an animal

Answer Key

page 4: fewer than 10 elephants

page 6: 9 feet

page 8: 4 meters

page 10: 8 feet

page 12: 3 feet

page 14: 2 inches

page 16: 2 meters

page 18: estimated sum = 20 elephants

page 20: estimated sum = 30 elephants

For More Information

Books

Bell, Samantha S. *Meet a Baby Elephant*. Minneapolis, MN: Lerner Publishing Group, 2016.

Hanson, Anders. *Elephant*. North Mankato, MN: ABDO Publishing Company, 2014.

Owens, Henry. *How to Track an Elephant*. New York, NY: Windmill Books, 2014.

Websites

African Elephant
kids.nationalgeographic.com/animals/african-elephant/
Check out more fun facts!

Asian Elephant
www.worldwildlife.org/species/asian-elephant
Find out how many are left and more.

Index